Town hall
—
Hilversum
—
W.M. Dudok

V+K Publishing / Inmerc

Colophon

Design

Jan Johan ter Poorten, José K. Vermeulen,
Cees de Jong, V+K Design, Naarden

Photography

Herman van Doorn, Soesterberg

Editor

Arjen Oosterman, Bussum

Grateful acknowledgement to

Max Cramer (Hilversum historic buildings committee)

G.W. van Hoogevest (project architect, Van Hoogevest
architecten BV)

R.M.H. Magnée (Dudok Foundation)

Jan Roest (chief inspector, Van Hoogevest architecten BV)

The Gooi en Vecht Regional Archive

Van Hoogevest architecten BV

Municipality of Hilversum

Hilversum Town hall

WM Dudok

© 1995 V+K Publishing / Inmerc, Naarden

ISBN 90 6611 434 7   NUGI 923

Acknowledgment

Unless otherwise stated, all drawings are courtesy of the
Dutch Architectural Institute. Archive pictures are courtesy
of the Gooi and Vecht Regional Archive.

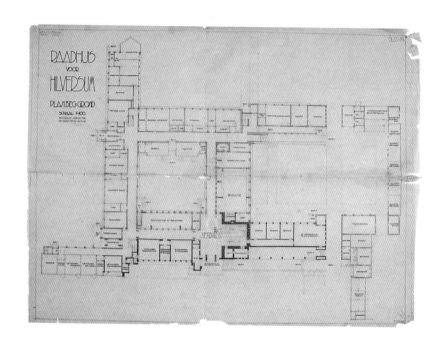

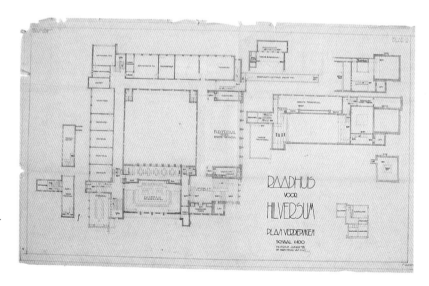

Contents

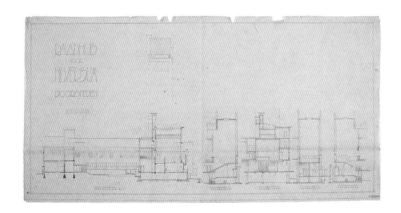

Titlepage: Perspective, final Town hall design, 'Witten Hull' site, [1924] Public Works Archive
Ground plan and cross-section, Town hall design, 'Witten Hull' site, January 1928, Public Works Archive

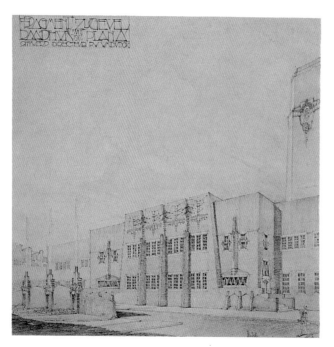

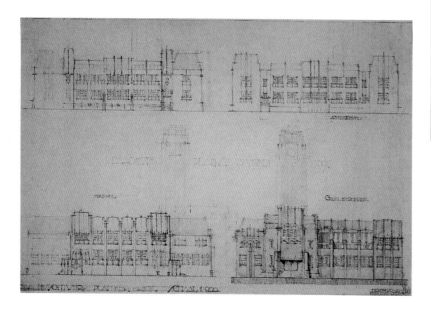

Side wall fragment, Kerkbrink Town hall design [Plan A],
June 1917

Views, Kerkbrink Town hall design [Plan A], January 1917

Perspective, Town hall design [Plan A], drawn by AH van
Wamelen, 1917

Perspective, Town hall design [Plan A], drawn by AH van
Wamelen, 1917

The 'supreme civic building':
an architectural jewel

1 For more detailed information on Dudok and his work, including literature on the town hall: H van Bergeijk, WILLEM MARINUS DUDOK, ARCHITECT-STEDE-BOUWKUNDIGE 1884-1974. Naarden (V+K Publishing) 1995. An interesting assessment of the town hall is: R. Garcia, 'Entre tradicim y vanguardia: Analisis del Ayuntomiento de Hilversum', in: ANALES DE ARQUITECTURA, 1992, no 4, pp 85-97, in which the layout is compared to that of El Escorial.

2 For the history of the old town hall: EE van Mensch et al, HET OUDE RAADHUIS TE HILVERSUM, Hilversum 1988.

3 Unless otherwise stated the quotations are from papers belonging to Hilversum City manager office archive stored in the Gooi and Vecht Regional Archive (SAGV).

Eighty years ago, Willem Marinus Dudok, newly appointed director of Hilversum council Public Works department, made his first design sketch for a new town hall. It was to be the start of a long drawn out design and building process. The vicissitudes of this project are described here, vicissitudes which elicited many a sigh from Dudok. That it was worth it is evident from the fact that the splendid yellow structure is not only the pinnacle of Dudok's œuvre but is among the pinnacles of twentieth-century architecture.[1]

Ever since the beginning of his career with the municipality of Hilversum, Dudok was more or less involved with the town hall's design. On his appointment it was under-stood that the designing of a new town hall was to be one of his most important assignments.[2] The old town hall was much too small and was threatening to burst at the seams. Even Dudok's own Public Works department suffered from this, to the slight irritation of its young director. *'While I've absolutely no desire to have luxury in an official department, for those assigned to work here I consider it not only impractical but its shabby interior is hardly inspiring, which no one would expect in a Municipality such as this.'*[3]

The first concept

The site for the new building was initially not a topic for discussion and did not pose a problem for Dudok. In his report to the council executive committee of 26 August 1915, he wrote: *'Ever since I've been with this Municipality, I've always envisaged the new Town hall at the Kerkbrink. The Kerkbrink has relatively no less a connotation for Hilversum than the Dam has for Amsterdam: it is the centre, an intersection for traffic, where all important routes converge or pass through, and thus it is there that the Municipality's most supreme civic building, from where the administrative duties for this Municipality emanate, should be sited. This site is therefore in keeping with the ideal connotation of a Town hall...Also from an urban planning viewpoint...is the building of a Town hall on this site an extremely worthwhile step'*. With his plan, Dudok also wanted to improve the traffic situation, which could have been the beginning of a gradual transformation of the inner city. The first time the architect visited Hilversum in 1915, he had been annoyed by the road between the station's square and Kerkbrink. He quickly lost his way and later he was told he had taken – what he ironically called – *'de koninklijke* weg' or royal way. This way, which as he himself contended – it even had no proper pavement at the time – was anything but fitting for the municipality.

The siting of the new building on Kerkbrink was carefully studied. 'The main front of the building comprises the western boundary of a very large square and should therefore have a decorative wall.' The building should also serve 'as a fitting culmination point of the townscape', the reason for having 'a dome or tower' above the main entrance which 'would provide a balance with the already existing structures on the Northerly side of the square'. Dudok took great care in creating 'a fine construction' for the freestanding building, which was not sited in the centre of the square, a position Dudok had considered as an earlier ground plan shows, but on the northwestern side. At the time an isolated siting of public monuments was regarded as unsuitable as they then became separated rather than interwoven with the urban structure. In his report of 30 August 1915, the appropriate responsible alderman proposed commissioning Dudok to work out his proposals and sub-mit these to a committee comprising PJH Cuypers and HP Berlage, the two fore-most Dutch architects of the day. The council formally gave him the commission on 1 September 1915. Dudok immediately set to work and over the next three months produced various sketches showing a range of architectural idiom, vary-ing from Berlage and Saarinen to the Amsterdam School. He often spent time tinkering particularly with the design for the dominant tower. The reason for the many alternatives was probably that he wanted to submit several designs to the committee hoping that at least one would prove popular. No committee however was ever set up.

During 1916 and 1917 Dudok worked on new designs for Kerkbrink and probably already on a plan for a piece of land belonging to a Mr Perk, a public notary, on 's-Gravelandseweg, which was also being considered as a possible site. For Kerkbrink – the spot he still preferred – Dudok chose a ground plan in the shape of a square. He tried several types of facade, the one sometimes more symmetrical than the other, though the tower was always placed asymmetrically. He did not consider an entirely symmetrical design desirable for two reasons. Firstly, the building would be sited at the intersection of two major streets and he felt this should be marked by the tower. Secondly, he did not think the square was wide enough for such a design solution. There was also the fact that by placing the tower asymmetrically, this would be situated further away from that of the city's Reformed Church. At the end of the summer of 1917, the plans were probably in their final stages and could be submitted to the council. The designs, which were in keeping with the Amsterdam School style – the one made in June 1917 is especially remarkable in that certain parts of the facade are designed as 'masks' – have a larger ground plan than Dudok's officially commissioned design of 1915. Notwithstanding, Jan Kardux, the City manager, was unhappy with the solution. The 1915 design had been worked out in narrow consultation with his

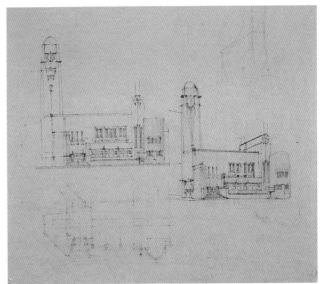

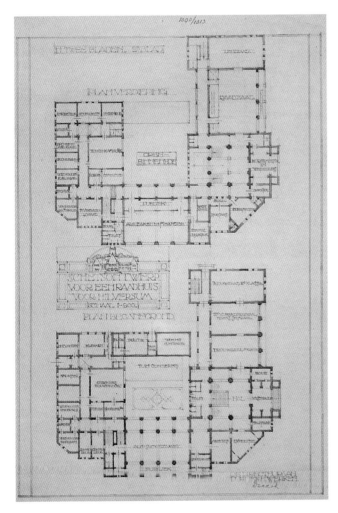

Ground plan, Kerkbrink Town hall design, [1915]

Town hall design sketches, March 1919

[8]

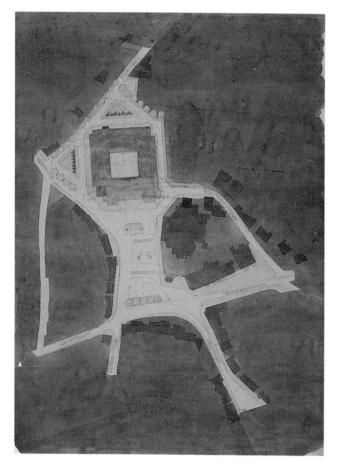

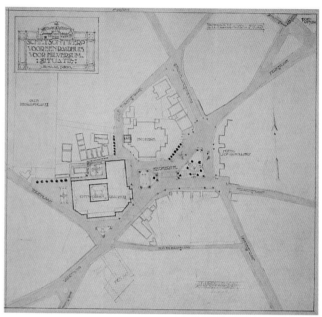

Site plan proposal, Kerkbrink Town hall design [Plan A],
January 1918

Site plan sketch, Kerkbrink Town hall design [Plan A], 1915

Site plan proposal, Kerkbrink Town hall design [Plan B],
January 1918

predecessor, J Mulder. However, when Kardux succeeded him in April 1917, he had reservations about the design concerning the spatial development and layout. He wanted drastic changes made and compiled a detailed list of wishes and criticisms, which were taken into account in the third design. This proposal, which was announced in a council report but which until now has never been identified, was labelled *'a bad German imitation'* by the local DE GOOI- EN EEMLANDER newspaper.

Dudok explained the new situation in a missive to the council executive committee on 12 November 1917: *'As an architect I feel obliged to take the view that I should not influence the client – this was the City manager for the most part – in his requirements; when someone assigns me that which is required then I fit in with this architectonically to the extent that these requirements are met as far as is possible. In as far as this is still needed, I would therefore like to point out that Mr Kardux's criticism does not apply to my proposals, nor the stated requirements at the time. Indeed I do not have the least objection to the new requirements Mr Kardux has developed as a motive for agreeing to a new proposal, but regard it professionally desirable that the Council declares itself in principle in agreement with this and commissions me to work out the plans in consultation with Mr Kardux. In this way, and as a follow-up to your earlier commission, the modifications are officially recorded and unnecessary work is prevented should the office of City manager again pass into another's hands before the building is completed. I have promptly and vigorously devoted myself to the new design and wish to inform you that I sincerely hope to be ready with this within four to six weeks, so that despite this hold up the council can take a decision in principle before the end of the year. Generally speaking I do not regret the huge amount of work I've carried out on these projects until now. Several projects are usually made for such buildings before the right one is arrived at, and the foregoing was certainly extremely useful from a scholarly viewpoint. I do not doubt that between Mr Kardux and myself there will be the same harmonious and enjoyable collaboration for this important work as was the case with the previous City manager, and regard the collaboration, which is only possible on such a scale when working in this way, as a foremost factor in order to achieve total success.'* The letter was intended to make sure that before the plans were submitted Dudok could be confident that the council would not be taken aback by the enormous changes.

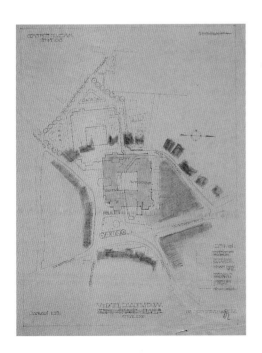

The site is deliberated

Shortly after this Dudok must have received assurance because at the end of 1917 he submitted three designs: a new Plan 'A' for a town hall on Kerkbrink, a Plan 'A/1' – also probably for Kerkbrink – that he did in collaboration with Kardux and a Plan 'B' for a town hall on *'s-Gravelandseweg*. On 8 January 1918 he held a talk in a closed council meeting outlining his plans in more detail. In response to the question:

'*Which is the most suitable site for the new Town hall*', he replied that Kerkbrink was the designated square for the town hall and quoted the appropriate extract from his first report. After criticising the possibility of siting the building on the north, south or east side of the square, he proposed designing it on the west side. '*Now you will undoubtedly remark that Kerkbrink is in no way what you'd call a beautiful square and that the buildings on that square are mainly such that they will for the most part sharply contrast with a monumental town hall. In the first instance it must be argued that Hilversum, unfortunately, hardly possesses entire areas that have architectural significance, so that a monumental building, at least in the built-up centre, will wind up in a less fortunate setting anywhere. We should not only regard the matter, however, from this pessimistic stand but take into account the enormous positive effect a Town hall building according to Plan 'A' will have on the entire environment. In order to realise this one should try to imagine from the site plan the drastic changes a Town hall in the heart of the municipality would create. Immediately evident is that Kerkbrink would be made a longer square in that it will gain almost twice its present length. The Western wall of the new square will be closed by the most decorative facade of the Town hall. It is also certain that via this square the building, when seen from the through road for visitors, will provide an unexpected sight. The building will have an even greater effect when you observe it after leaving the Kerkstraat, for the distribution of mass in the square facade is such that the highest point is situated in the longitudinal axis of Kerkstraat, and a restrained yet decorative tower for this street will crown the general townscape. An observer approaching Kerkbrink from Heerenstraat will be afforded a similar sort of view. These are the considerations which led me in this case, on the grounds of urban planning requirements of the area, not to seek a symmetrical solution for the Town Hall project according to Plan A, however much I generally regard the symmetry of monumental buildings as being important.*' To underpin his preference for Kerkbrink from an urban planning viewpoint, Dudok referred to Raymond Unwin's book, TOWN PLANNING IN PRACTICE, published in 1909. He quoted a long extract from the book relating to Camillo Sitte's theory that buildings work better when they are not isolated. After this explanation, he went into the siting of a building on 's Gravenlandseweg. The site on this road, however, did not really form a coherent whole with the town plan. It might have been broad and attractive but '*important main roads did not converge on it, you soon even realise there is something unnatural about this position in that you feel the building stands somewhat to the side, in fact, of where it organically should be*'. The site did provide more architectonic possibilities: '*...while with Plan A one can aspire to a logical distribution of mass as well as monumentality, the latter aspect can be much better expressed according to Plan B due to sufficient frontage being available here to provide a solution which in its essence readily brings us much closer to monumentality, viz the symmetrical solution. The nature of the Town hall building as an administrative centre is conveyed in this plan by grouping all its parts around a dominant central building from which the tower rises high as a crowning ele-*

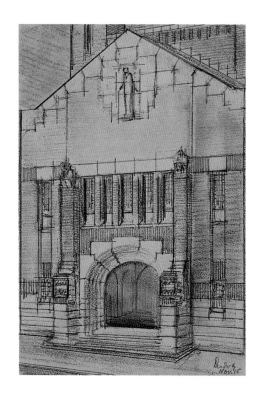

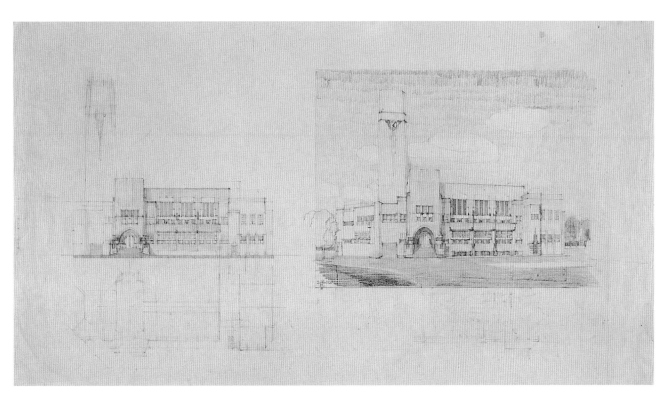

Entrance perspective, Kerkbrink Town hall design,
November 1915
Kerkbrink Town hall design, ca 1917/1918

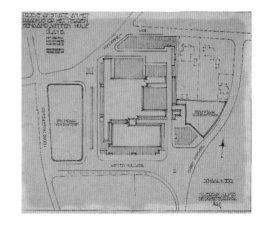

Site plan proposal, Kerkbrink Town hall design [Plan A],
January 1918
Site plan, 'Witten Hull' Town hall design, July 1923
Site plan, 'Perk' Town hall design, July 1923

ment. Its low, greatly protruding wings on either side culminate in small, massive extensions enclosed by a simple yet decorative garden landscaping which, with its monumental driveway and two side approaches converging at the main entrance, is entirely in keeping with the Town hall's architectural style.' The local DE GOOI- EN EEMLANDER newspaper thought, however, that the Perk plan had the least to recommend it: 'a splen-did townscape cannot be gained from that point, at most only a sort of palace-like view'.

Town planning considerations led Dudok to declare a preference for Plan A, though the architectonic ones he felt were in Plan B's favour. The council executive committee preferred Plan A, while most of Hilversum's residing architects, including C de Groot and JW Hanrath, were still not convinced that the 'right place' had been found.

Although the executive committee declared itself against organising an architectural competition to obtain a useable design for the town hall and thought Dudok 'had proved himself as a competent architect' a few voices were still heard in favour of holding a competition. The Dutch Architects Association was of the opinion that 'such works should be designed and led by independently working and highly qualified architects'. That architecture should not be centralised 'within a municipal department'. Public Works was in essence a maintenance service. The local DE GOOI- EN EEMLANDER newspaper held a questionnaire among architects but opinion was divided. During a three-hour council meeting on the building on 19 March 1918, Councillor Bakker defended the choice of Dudok and argued that he had in fact been appointed in order to find a design solution for important matters of this kind. Up until that moment Dudok had met all expectations and was regarded as a 'young, sensitive and talented architect'. Moreover the problem of the town hall was closely linked to that concerning a development scheme, which in fact was more important. As one councillor concluded after a lengthy deliberation: 'Where we on behalf of the municipality of Amsterdam have dared assign such an important plan as the development scheme to the director of Public Works – and the partial modifications he has already made in that plan show he has an extremely clear view of this and a huge talent – then we can also confidently assign him to design the new Town hall'. The result of this testimony was that the council supported the executive committee's proposal. The council's financial difficulties and the problems surrounding the buying of a suitable site, however, led to nothing coming of the building for the time being. Moreover, there was no unanimity on a suitable building site. As numerous sketches reveal, Dudok continued to work on a design for Kerkbrink until 1922. On 5 September of that same year the council decided to set up a fund for the building of a new town hall and to purchase the Witten Hull estate. It argued: 'Together with the Public Works committee and the director of Public Works we are of the opinion that this is an eminently suitable site on which to build a town hall, that it meets all requirements and that it fits

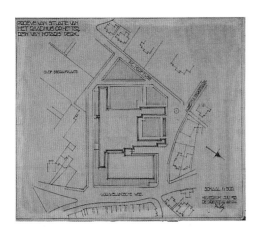

both into our garden village as well as into the immediate environment. The site is situated in the heart of the garden village. While certain access roads may be too narrow these can easily be made wider...' With that the debate entered a new phase.

The final choice of site

The new mayor of Hilversum, Paul Reymer, was the driving force behind the matter of a town hall from the very beginning and under his guidance a solution was eventually to be found. When the council asked Dudok to make a report on the possible location of the new town hall, he once more set to work, so that several sketches of the town hall, especially of the south front, exist from the latter part of 1922. They show him continuing along the same route he had already taken with his designs for the Rembrandt and Bavinck schools, though the expressiveness of the brickwork was less marked. The town hall building had to express itself in particular through the composition of its masses. The influence of Jan Wils, with whom Dudok thought of setting up a practice in The Hague at the time, is also evident. In his sketches Dudok paid much attention to defining the boundaries of the various faces, to penetrating the blocks and to a balanced grouping of the masses. The massive tower formed the focal point of the composition, which not only marked the entrance but also indicated that the building had to be approached from *Melkpad* along *Oude Enghweg*. This is not only the pinnacle of the entire design, but also the dominant feature in constructing the most important south front, behind which the official spaces were situated. This main facade was increasing straightened until it was a three-dimensional screen with a large pond in front. The lower side wings were extensions of the south front. In order to make the screen larger and namely higher, Dudok raised the wall face of the council chamber more and on its roof even placed a false wall face, which aside from its aesthetic appeal had no other function. From the accompanying explanation to the design, Dudok increasingly visualised the town hall as an important backdrop, a fitting background for celebratory occasions. The architecture was to be a *mise en scène*.

On 4 January 1923 Dudok submitted a weighty missive in which he wrote: *'On the assumption that I still regard my earlier considerations as being still generally correct, I cannot deny that further considerations and architectural experience have not been without their influence on my attitude towards this matter in the sense that I do not expect a satisfactory outcome from erecting a Town hall on Kerkbrink in the manner as was indicated at the time...the Town hall will not be able to save this unattractive square in an aesthetic sense and conversely the square would do serious harm to the aesthetic effect of the erected building'*. He also pointed out the costs that expropriation would incur. The lack of economic freedom to recreate *Kerkbrink* entirely would result in the town hall having a *'relatively cramped position'*. Regarding *'s-Gravelandseweg*, he argued that this

Final Town hall design, 'Witten Hull' site, [1924]

Final Town hall design, 'Witten Hull' site, [1924]
Final Town hall design, 'Witten Hull' site, [1924]

was 'undoubtedly the main route through our village of villas and in the most dignified manner brings out the nature of our Municipality as a flourishing garden village. The site belonging to Notary Perk (that was offered for sale a few years ago) also has the advantage of being mainly in the centre of the built environment. Though it is not particularly large, it is still big enough to make a resplendent extension of the building in the form of a monumental garden possible, which will greatly benefit the total aspect'. Dudok made the nature of Hilversum as a garden village the starting point of his new design. This also had to radiate from the town hall itself. 'More and more I conceive of the Town hall in our garden village as a monumental yet, at the same time, romantic structure in a garden, rising above beautiful lawns, surrounded and decorated with trees and flowers and with everything that extremely ornamental landscaping can achieve.'

Meanwhile Perk was unwilling to negotiate further with the council concerning a sale. In a letter dated 4 September 1922, he wrote 'I'm too much attached to the spot to voluntarily leave the property'. Another alternative had to be therefore considered. Another site that had been under discussion was the country house 'Vogelenzang' (Birdsong) belonging to the Blijdensteyn family, also situated on the 's-Gravelandseweg. This could only be partly built on, however, as the remainder had to be used as a public park. As for the 'attractively cultivated complex' on Witten Hullweg that the council could buy for 234.000 guilders, Dudok thought it 'undoubtedly an opportunity to build a Town hall in a beautiful, rural setting, but it had the disadvantage of only being accessible along relatively narrow roads. The important centre that could arise here in this manner would then not be connected to the remaining road network to the same important degree'. Dudok argued that the area on Witten Hullweg was still the most suitable as it was a sort of compromise among all the other options: not too remote and in a beautiful setting. Dudok had the Public Work committee's support, though one member still thought a new town hall should be built in the centre of the Municipality 'on Kerkbrink where virtually all major thoroughfares converge and where the proposed building could be an embodiment of itself'. The building could also be coupled to improving the most prominent square of the village. Referring to the narrow roads, in November 1927 Dudok argued that a town hall did not belong 'to buildings which draw huge crowds at certain times of the day or into which a stream of people suddenly enters, as is the case with stations, exhibition halls, theatres and so on'.

There did have to be sufficient space, however, for cars to draw up and park. Nevertheless, the architect was still aware that the solution was not ideal. He thought it sensible 'to keep the option open for a later generation to make an access road that met all the requirements'. With a few sketches he illustrated how this could be done.

The final design

While the choice of site appeared to have been made, Dudok did not entirely rule out the option of a building on 's-Gravelandsweg as a site plan from July 1923 shows. This plan is virtually identical to that made for the *Witten Hull* site, made in the same month. At the end of the month the council decided to buy *Witten Hull* as well as properties 1 and 3 on *Wittenhullweg*. Shortly after, on 5 September 1923, the executive committee commissioned him to design proposals *'with all possible speed'* for a town hall that was to be built on the *Wittenhullweg* site. On 4 June 1924 he submitted the proposals, of which the 24 drawings *'when studied would be able to provide a formal impression of the internal and external forms of the building'*. In the accompanying explanation he pointed out *'that in a site drawing for a modern structure, planning and building are inextricably linked to each other.*

There is no difference whatsoever in aesthetic value between ground plan and facade; each one of them is only a flat projection of the three-dimensional whole. The distribution of the various spaces, the manner and form of the grouping, is also governed from the outset not only by practical requirements but every bit as much by the envisaged aesthetic effect'. About the building itself he said: *'It rises above the middle of relatively extensive parkland; the architecture is carried over into a monumental landscaped garden; the supreme civic building in our municipality, with its open position and setting, thus reflects the nature of our municipality as a garden village. From every side of the building one has more than sufficient distance to gain a complete, clear impression. For the building's main entrance, the South front, a pond is envisaged; the building will therefore rise out of the water'*. The idea of a large pond reflecting the townhall was most likely inspired by a study trip made to Gothenburg in 1923, where Dudok probably visited the international urban development exhibition as well as Stockholm and Copenhagen. In Stockholm he had the opportunity to visit the townhall built by Ragnar Ostberg between 1911 and 1923.[4] The pond also had a particular function. *'This will enhance the sense of splendour to the most official part of the townhall – then on formal or ceremonial occasions one will particularly gain an impression of this when approaching the building by the pond and seeing it reflected in the water. The building does not suddenly ascend, but with its lower wings seeks an alliance, as it were, with the surrounding landscaped garden. Moreover, these lower wings anchor the building, as it were, in the remaining indistinguishable form of the building plot's northern boundary.'*

When dealing with the official space he namely draws attention to the solution for the main entrance *'which provides access for council members and invited guests of council meetings, for formal town hall receptions and also for marriage ceremonies. On such occasions a procession of people converge on the townhall and that is why, in an aesthetic sense, this entrance has been built. One drives along the main access road along the pond's Eastern boundary and alights at the Southern open entrance between both parts of the building. One then walks along the pond to the main entrance, either under the covered*

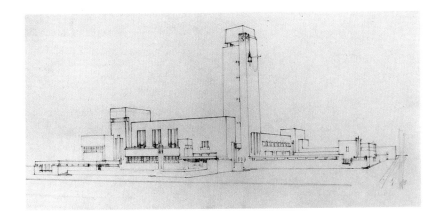

Town hall design, 'Witten Hull' site, [1922] [19]

Town hall design, 'Witten Hull' site, [1923]

Town hall design, 'Witten Hull' site, [1923]

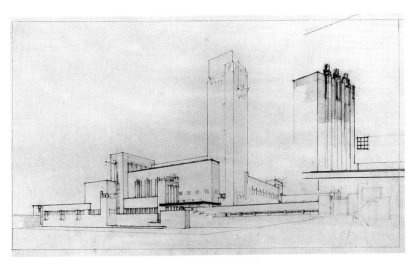

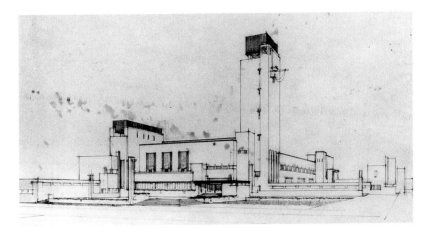

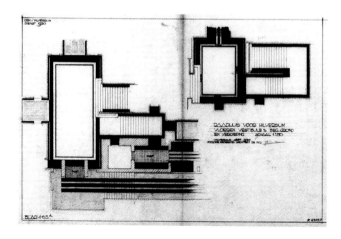

Final design, Council Chamber interior
Initial drawing of entrance hall floors on the ground and
first floor, September 1930

colonnade in bad weather, or along the uncovered way. Ahead is a broad, monumental flight of steps under a grand, shady awning leading to the spacious vestibule. From here one directly reaches, without going through an inner porch, the central hall via its grand main doors. Along this route there is not anything to disturb the splendid approach to the building. The general public can easily be kept at a distance and from the other side of the pond can watch the procession approaching the building; no impeding swinging doors interrupt the advancing movement. On those occasions during very bad weather when the need for a covered entrance is felt, a porch at the end of the colonnade is planned which gives immediate access to the main staircase and hall. This hall is relatively low (around 4m) but the greater the effect when one ascends the main staircase and suddenly makes out a 16m high space above one. This main staircase harmonises with the entire concept of the structure and also with the free layout of the official rooms leading off: designed asymmetrically with a double-flight arrangement. I'm convinced that the contrast between the only one floor high, easy to ascend staircase and the large space developed above it will create an enormous impression. The staircase is conceived in black marble with a light blue-green runner; the lower part of the staircase walls with black marble panelling contrasting with the white marble panelling planned for the entry porch.' Dudok sought 'strong alternating impressions' and 'highly contrasting effects of light, volume and forms'.

On the architecture itself Dudok said: 'From the various perspective drawings you will see I've remained faithful to an architectural view that has manifest itself in the various buildings I've designed until now for the council. I have attempted to attain the monumentality appropriate for a townhall, but at the same time to preserve a rural character. The latter is by no means linked to the concept of a thatched roof, the rural character is expressed here, in my view, through the building gradually ascending above its setting and through the intimate interweaving of garden and structure, the severity of which needs the contrast of a luxuriant garden. The architectural impact rests exclusively on the effect of the volumes and the interrelationship of the various parts of the building, on their mutual affinity and antithesis to each other. Windows and doors are therefore the most obvious decorative elements of the wall faces. In a modern office building no significant roof space is necessary: I have thus adopted modern means for the flat roofing thereby dispensing with the undoubtedly highly decorative ones for which high roof facing lends itself. On the other hand if there were no other aesthetic possibilities, then the acceptance of this so-called flat building, no matter how practically justifiable, would undoubtedly mean a backward step artistically speaking. I feel, however, that this flat building does in fact contain a characteristic option which need not lose out aesthetically to visible roofing: I mean the option of a highly pronounced silhouette effect. The aesthetics of the steep roof lies in its restful, secure covering and its beauty shows up best when, with the greatest simplicity, without any complicated forms, it rests on the building like a blanket, while adopting flat roofing gives the freedom to cover various parts of the building at different levels and gives it an interesting silhouette. I have attempted to employ this characteristic effect here, *and I think it has greatly enhanced the structure from whatever point it is observed. Immediately at the main entrance one is struck by the huge contrast between the low entrance colonnade and the massive tower rising up behind. According to tradition the church and the town hall have always had a tower; I think it is good to follow this tradition. This tower not only has the main, ascending staircase but has also been so built that it is embellished with a set of bells…Moreover I wish to point out that this tower, despite the asymmetrical arrangement of the entire design, is nevertheless the central dominating apex of the building from any angle. The various perspective drawings make this clear; they also demonstrate how the building, in contrast to symmetrical Renaissance buildings, provides a different aspect from every side, even though it has the same overall character throughout. These changing images, the one seen from high building masses across lower facades, that constant juxtaposing of those building parts in relation to each other as the viewer moves, the so-called 'coulisse' effect, that is a three-dimensional opulence after all and achieved by pure architectural means. Putting aside the constantly shifting fads and fashions, I have tried, as it were, to focus on the essence of architecture, and to work only with that which has always been the core of architectural beauty. No lavish detailing, but lavish volume effects and a grand presence will be the hallmarks of this structure. By this I do not wish to deny the value of detailing. I certainly wish to apply the necessary refinements at certain points, as a contrast to the large building masses. Under the colonnade I envisage a brightly coloured tile covering, blue with a hint of gold, with a similar sort of covering in a lighter colour continuing across the ceiling. For the main entrance awning I thought of lining the underside with white marble, inlaid with strips of black marble. I propose crowning the front extension's three brick structures, which support the awning on the lefthand side, with a monumental piece of sculpture depicting Authority between Justice and the Law.'*

To illustrate his point, Dudok made several design projections of the sculpture. Light is further admitted into the entry porch via a sequence of small windows just above the awning, a solution that Jan Wils, among others, had used for his *Papaverhof* building in The Hague. It is interesting that Dudok does not refer to colour. His small designs were not coloured in, so it is unclear when, precisely, he chose yellow for the brickwork. Dudok had tried various types of brickwork in experimental walls, but not one was found suitable *'because in the way they were joined they formed an unrestful whole for the eyes'*. Only by using a different brick pattern and way of joining could *'a satisfactory choice'* finally be made. For the building of the town hall, the architect had a special sized, yellow brick fired, which was smaller and longer than the standard one, the so-called Hilversum brick measuring 23.3 x 4.3 x 11.3 cm and produced by Alfred Russel, a firm in Tegelen. In November 1928 some 610,000 bricks were ordered. This custom-made brick, together with the building's blue highlights, provided a cheerful colour that was remarked upon by everyone. As the architect admitted in a letter to Sverre Poulsen, editor of a Nordic journal, Byggekunst, he attached much importance to the *Farbenwirkung*.

The main/First wedding room under [23]
construction [Hilversum Public Works]
Entrance to the courtyard

Photograph taken during construction, ca 1930

[Hilversum Public Works]

He consciously sought *die nötige Farbengegenstellung* so that his buildings both in winter and summer *'noch genugsam unterhaltend und "farbenfreudig" sind'*, especially when it is cloudy.[5] The yellow colour prompted the architect HF Sijmons to write: *The natural position of this house is reminiscent of a reclining lion'.*[6]

In a letter of 8 May 1924 to the Willink family, for whom Dudok had designed a villa in Hengelo in 1921, the architect disclosed what the council's executive committee thought about his town hall design. *'The Mayor thought it was more like a fort than a Town hall. The City manager thought it was more beautiful than the Berlage Stock Exchange, though he thought the Exchange was downright ugly. One of the councillors complimented me; he thought it was an outstanding project but expected that it would create a storm of protest among the general public, who would undoubtedly find it exceptionally ugly.'*[7] The density of the south front, behind which the mayor's quarters and the council chamber were located – and where meetings were mainly held in the evenings – betrayed Dudok's training at the Royal Military Academy in Breda. In order to make the design more known nationally and thus to put pressure on the council, the architect arranged for it to be published in the arts journal WENDINGEN at about the same time he was due to submit it. The council, however, considered postponing the building and also thought of looking for yet another site while selling the one on the *Witten Hullweg*. Fifty-five, mainly well-known architects reacted to this by sending a protest to the council in which they urged *'the decision taken by the council on 31 July 1923 to be upheld and should the realisation, through adverse circumstances, be objected to now, then in which case to propose that the Council postpones the Town Hall building until a more favourable time, while retaining, however, the designated site and accepting the design in principle.'* It was Berlage in particular who appointed himself as a defender of a design in which he could recognise both his classical and pictorial concepts. The impact the design had on Berlage is namely reflected in his modified designs for the Gemeentemuseum in The Hague. The plans for the town hall were exhibited in the gym of a local secondary school on the Rembrandtlaan in Hilversum so that everyone could get acquainted with the design.

The writer Antoon Coolen summed up his opinion on the town hall as follows: *'There is not one dominant facade. There are numerous facets which brings the entire construction to life and which are revealed time and again, depending on the angle from which you view the whole, it is pure and genuine vitality, a game, a continuous as well as surprising interplay of volumes, an entire symphony of plasticity achieved purely by architectural means, based on the core principle of all architecture: functional logic and beauty.'*

On 25 November 1924 Dudok's design was accepted by the council, but due to financial constraints the start of the building was postponed. This was a new disappointment for the architect, who had already written earlier to FR Willink, director of the Heemaffabriek, a firm in Hengelo: *'The economic misery also causes great*

5 Letter dated 6 November 1931, in: DUDOK COLLECTION FOUNDATION.

6 HF Sijmons, 'Het nieuwe Raadhuis', in: DE GOOI- EN EEMLANDER, 1924, no 50, p 1.

7 Letter in: the DUDOK ARCHIVE (DA) OF THE DUTCH ARCHITECTURAL INSTITUTE (NAI), Portfolio 38FM14.

8 From: Council proceedings, 25 November 1924.

9 'Een nieuw bedrijf "Raadhuisbouw"', De Gooi- en Eemlander, 24 February 1928, no 47, p 1.

10 For information on the first year of the building: the town hall building diary in: the Dudok archive of the Dutch Architectural Institute, box 47.

disappointment in my life. I have made a design for a Town hall with which I have had a lot of success among my colleagues. I also had many expectations of this and it would have the same implications for my career as Berlage's Stock Exchange for his. It is perhaps the only really monumental work I will get to make! And now there is much campaigning to prevent it being built due to the hard times'. Following on from this, he continued: 'We Dutch are not an ostentatious loving race that has much time for beauty such as the Swedes or the Danes'. The council declared itself in favour of Dudok's design. Only a few councillors had certain criticisms such as Councillor De Vries. He argued that 'whatever style is used for the building, be it Byzantine, Romanticism, Cubist or Futuristic, the appearance of the erected building should be in keeping with its function'. According to him this was not the case. 'When the Council receives guests, welcoming them on the Municipality's behalf, then people want to see this but this is only possible when the front of the Town hall has a broad ascending, highly visible entrance. You have to look for the entrance in Mr Dudok's design: you have to turn two 90 degree corners to find the entrance tucked behind a wall.' Councillor Bierman was another one who felt that Hilversum did not need a 'resounding town hall' like Amsterdam or Sweden had. 'If you build a Town hall in such a way that people come from far and wide to admire the building and to see the pond illuminated in the evening than that would have ensuing neg-ative effects for the municipality's development.'[8] The council finally decided to post-pone the building for two years and it was only in November 1927 that they felt ready to start building. In October 1927 a weekly architectural magazine Bouwkundig Weekblad Architectura had published an issue in which numerous architects stated their recommendations. A few months later, in February 1928, a new municipal body was founded, the Raadhuisbouw or Town hall building, which was briefed to organise and monitor the running of things, as well as being respon-sible for the accounts.[9]

As with many other Hilversum buildings, the town hall was built to keep the costs down. In 1924 Dudok had given an estimate of 1 115 000 guilders; in 1927, 1 156 000 guilders (contracted out) or 1 058 000 (under own management). After a beginning had been made on 26 March 1928 with fencing off and erecting site huts at Witten Hull, it was only on 31 July 1931 that the building could officially be used. The long building time was to blame, among others, on a severe frost during the winter of 1929. In April of that same year the construction workers had also threatened strike action if they did not get a pay increase.[10] The total costs had risen to 1 263 000 guilders. Dudok justified the higher amount by pointing out that the building 'indeed is more expensive but in point of fact considerably more has been added than was originally envisaged'. The interior was more fireproof, the costs for installing electricity had greatly exceeded the estimate and many spare rooms had to be furnished in order to be used for meetings. He stressed the point, however, that he had aimed to be as restrained as possible 'concerning both the rational organ-isation of the building programme as well as in the simple, yet meticulous detailing in

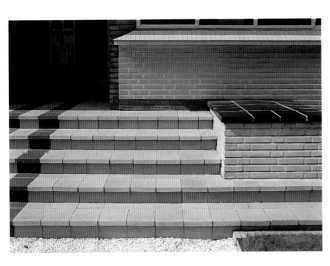

Two views of the side wall and courtyard entrance,
restored Town hall

West wall, south wall and view from the southwest,
restored Town hall

every part of the building'. Dudok also economised on materials though he always looked for *'very durable materials and used extremely hard-wearing constructions'* again in order to keep maintenance costs down as much as possible. The windowsills which he initially wanted in Swedish granite were later made from black glazed ceramic tiles.

11 *Letter in:* the Dudok archive of the Dutch Architectural Institute, 53M11

12 C Veth, *'Het Hilversumse Raadhuis', in:* Maandblad voor Beeldende Kunsten, 1932, no 1, p 14.

Praise and criticism

Many Dutch architects had already seen the work before the town hall opened and expressed their admiration. AH Wegerif wrote to the architect on 17 May: *'This is something so beautiful, something from a better, more beautiful world suddenly set down before us'.*[11]

One of those who put a damper on the rejoicing was Ben Merkelbach, who wrote: *'Whenever we ask ourselves what significance this building has for the development of architecture, then the important question is whether there is that much cause for jubilation'.* According to him it was hardly functionalist in style and therefore *'was not modern in spirit'.* While he admitted that it had a certain monumentality, he added *'In the future its monumentality will help us very little'.* He saw the building as something from a fairy tale in which the councillors could perhaps imagine themselves at home, but in which the average user feels lost. Merkelbach's criticism was echoed, though in different words, by architect C Veth a few months later. Although he thought the building had an *'excellent layout'* he found it still objectionable as a whole. The facades in particular had to bear the brunt of his criticism. *'We stand before what is from beginning to end a stage set aimed at effect, it is such precise work that any effect of life on it instantly creates a blot. Pipes, window rails, everything has been hidden away in deference to the lines of the building. Only rows of flower pots are allowed on windowsills, which in themselves contribute little to enhancing the facade'*[12] For the conservative-minded Veth this town hall was *'an ingenious complex of secretive brick volumes with mysterious observation posts and concealed corridors and not the accessible accommodation of government'.* It is possible, however, that Veth had focused too much on the south front, a side which could conjure up associations with a castle. The west front, however, where the public entrances are, reflects little of the density of the main facade.

Architect Van der Steur, despite certain criticism – he felt the building's architectural climax was already reached before entering the main reception hall – was full of praise for the building in a talk he gave. He argued that *'Dudok's work indeed lived up to its promise, which we recognised when he made his design public seven or eight years ago. It says quite a lot if we can say today that a building plan is not yet outdated after so many years. And that during those years – even with*

13 C Blotkamp, 'Mondriaan-architectuur', in: MONDRIAAN IN DETAIL, Utrecht/Antwerp 1987, p 84.

14 W Holzbauer, 'W.M. Dudok – Town Hall, Hilversum, Netherlands, 1928-31', in: GLOBAL ARCHITECTURE, no 58, Tokyo, 1981.

15 ibid.

16 Letter from Dudok, dated 6 November 1931, to Sverre Poulsen, publisher of BYGGEKUNST magazine (Dudok Collection Foundation).

the influences that have obviously been incorporated – it has not lost its unity shows that the creator's work developed in conjunction with himself and his period throughout that time.' The building, however, had developed more in conjunction with Dudok being given more authority: the quarters for Public Works had increased considerably and as Town Architect he now had his own room. He also wanted an extra spare drawing office *'which can be used for drawing up development schemes and building contractor designs'.*

After more than 60 years, Hilversum town hall is still one of the most remarkable buildings and is also admired by the broad general public. In his accompanying lengthy explanation of his design, Dudok himself wrote: *'I do not count on this building being immediately popular, but what important building has ever enjoyed widespread popularity as soon as it was completed? It is the same with architecture as it often is with people with character: only a few recognise this quality right away; most recognise it later'.* The architect was right up to a point. As has already been said, Merkelback, a functionalist, did not think the building modern, a view also shared by Piet Mondrian, who thought the building *'quasi-modern'*, in his eyes it was *'the old in a new form'.*[13]

In view of the importance Dudok attached to the timeless quality of architecture, he would have taken Mondrian's remark as a compliment. The majority of his contemporaries recognised the Hilversum architect's achievement. Sometimes they had certain reservations and thought it fell short on certain points, but admitted that it more than exceeded expectations. The public at large could also identify with the building. According to W Holzbauer its appreciation lay in the fact that the building was the answer *'to the longings of the people for a modern architecture with traditional values, such as composition, fine craftsmanship and noble materials and, last but not least, a sense of monumentality'.*[14]

The same was maintained by Maristella Casciato when she wrote that Dudok has *'a method of working in which a view of architecture as rationally free composition is blended with one in which it is seen as attention to and assimilation of common values, of formal messages that are new but ready to be accepted and understood by the majority'.*[15]

The building has now been restored to its original glory. We can still argue about whether it is beautiful or ugly, a fairytale castle or a bunker, its interior cold, cool or chilly. Meanwhile it cannot be denied that it has become an intrinsic part of the history of modern architecture; a jewel in Hilversum's modern architectural crown. In order to understand that, the building should be seen, not from illustrations, but in reality. You should walk around and through the building in order to experience its spaciality. As Dudok wrote: *'Architektur kann man eigentlich nie aus Bilder ersehen: Architektur muss man erleben'.*[16] Since his arrival in Hilversum Dudok knew that the town hall would be the pinnacle of his career and that he should not try to equal it. A few years after the building's completion,

*South wall from Dudok's office, detail of the pinnacle of
the tower and view from the south, restored Town hall*

The Council Chamber and the Council Chamber with
council executive committee table, restored Town hall

he wrote that he was increasingly looking for a simplification of form *'for in art it comes down to simplicity and it is strange that it takes a lifetime to reach the minimal. The most pronounced and lasting effect is not achieved with abundant means but with extreme restrictions'*.[17] This simplifying of form resulted in the composition of his later buildings being more transparent, while the sculptural effect, achieved through penetrating the building volumes, disappeared altogether. It is precisely its remarkable composition that makes the town hall a unique building and which the architect was able to oversee down to the last detail while it was being built. He also made designs for the interiors of certain rooms, the furniture and colour schemes. From a monumental viewpoint, it competes with foreign town halls by Ragnar Ostberg in Stockholm, Hermann Billing in Kiel and Wilhelm Kreis in Herne and in the Netherlands, for instance, by Henri Evers in Rotterdam and G Firedhoff in Enschede. As H T Wijdeveld wrote in a letter to Dudok on 1 July 1949: *'You grasped beauty and bestowed on our country a world of form that makes us feel happy. Where your works arise, the environment starts singing'*.[18] And undoubtedly the town hall is a joyful building.

[33]

17 WM Dudok, 'Gedachten over Stedebouw en Bouwkunst. Toelichting door voorbeelden uit mijn practijk', in: Bouwkunst, Stedebouw, Dekoratieve Kunsten, *1935, no 11, p 333.*
18 Letter in: the Dudok archive of the Dutch Architectural Institute, *box 43.*

[34]   *The Reception Room, restored Town hall*

Restoration

The municipality of Hilversum took over ten years to restore its famous town hall and to have it in optimum condition once more. More problematical than the partial rebuilding was the funding of this extensive and costly project.

Fifty years after being built Hilversum town hall showed series defects. The building was shabby, the technical installations were outdated and the offices did not conform to current standards. In order to do something about this, Van Hoogevest, an architectural practice in Amersfoort drew up an extensive restoration plan based on retaining Dudok's concept as far as possible. This had far-reaching consequences, for Dudok had been involved with just about everything to do with the town hall, ranging from the geraniums in the courtyard, the furniture, lamps and interiors to the designing of the surrounding environment.

The cost of restoring, including the interior and garden, was estimated at 32 million guilders. Where the money for this ambitions project was to come from was unclear for a long time: you can't get blood out of a stone, or in this case two stones. On the one hand, the the municipality of Hilversum was supposed to foot a significant part of the bill. Hilversum, however, had not been able to balance its budget for years and as a so-called 'Article 12 council' had been threatened for some time with being placed under government legal restraint. On the other, there was entitlement to a substantial contribution from the state funded Historic Buildings Conservation Department but that was an even more dire situation. According to regulations the state contributed a fixed percentage of the restora -tion costs of listed buildings, but for many years demand had far outstripped resources. This meant in practice that it was the exception to the rule that a grant was awarded. This time, however, Hilversum was successful. The council chose for quality and refused to compromise. With each new restoration phase the necessary millions of guilders were coughed up, sometimes in a miraculous way.

The success of the restoration proves that aspiring to quality, even under difficult circumstances, can pay-off. Noblesse Oblige. Working from the splendidly restored 'supreme civic building' Hilversum council now has to get seriously down to overseeing Dudok's largest 'art work': the urban development scheme for a suburb of 100,000 inhabitants. Partly due to Dudok, Hilversum became the 'new historic town' of the Netherlands. Its lively and rich legacy, which has too easily been dismissed as a problem, offers Hilversum the opportunity to promote itself as an ideal place to live and work – at least if this is done sensibly enough.

The diagnosis

The story of the town hall's restoration begins in 1984 when DHV, a firm of consulting engineers in Amersfoort, were commissioned by the council to conduct a survey into the technical condition of the building. The report was perfectly clear: only a radical restoration could halt the building's deterioration. The walls revealed serious frost damage because the bricks at the time had not been fired hard enough and easily broke as they froze. The slanting construction joints which created horizontal shadow lines in the walls, and are known as 'Dudok joints' made it easy for rainwater to penetrate the brickwork. Moreover the walls could not dilate, or in other words seams that could absorb the expanding and contracting of the material as a result of shifts in temperature. Even the rainwater pipes were disastrous for the brickwork. Dudok had bricked these cast-iron pipes into the wall out of sight. As they started to rust they broke straight through the wall. They were also clogged because during summer gravel and bitumen from the roof melted and remained lodged in the pipes.

It was immediately apparent that the brickwork of the walls had to be more or less replaced as did the steel window frames, the tiles and tiled floors. The tower was in such a bad state that the upper part had to be completely rebuilt. Even concrete decay had took hold. Through insufficient covering the reinforcement of the concrete was rusting in many places. Altogether there was a long list of assorted things found wanting, such as ventilation in the lavatories and protection against lightening.

The ministry responsible for historic buildings conservation did not at all welcome a costly restoration. It also appeared to be an impossible task. The cultural minister at the time, Elco Brinkman, was more enthusiastic and pledged a grant for the first million guilders. The time was thus ripe for concrete plans to be made for the restoration. In 1986 the present-day firm of Van Hoogevest Architects BV were assigned this task. The firm was chosen, among others, for its wide experience with restoration work, including the medieval churches in Utrecht. It was also considered capable of keeping the costs of such a complex restoration under control.

The project

In Van Hoogevest's proposal putting right the town hall's shortcomings and construction faults without damaging the aesthetic merit came obviously to the fore. The way this should be approached, in contrast to numerous other restoration projects, elicited little debate. Dudok's signature is so forcefully evident in every detail of the town hall that to think of contrasting additions or drastic changes

The Wedding Room, restored Town hall

The courtyard with pond and the west side entrance,

restored Town hall

was already ruled out in advance. Fortunately the building had always retained its original function and there was surprisingly much of the interior and furnishings still intact. Broadly speaking the town hall still functioned in the way it had been intended, with an official part (wedding hall, reception hall, council chamber), offices (council services) and back-up facilities (technical spaces, storage, maintenance). The necessary changes, such as providing better access for the disabled, could easily be designed in an appropriate style. Virtually all the design elements which had been lost were accurately reconstructed from old photographs, sketches, on-the-spot surveys or oral history.

The less the basic approaches to the restoration gave cause for debate, the more they created practical worries. First of all it was hard to trace or reproduce the original building materials, which for the most part had been specially made for the town hall. It was also an entire *tour de force* to develop the appropriate technical modifications without marring the look of the building. The time scale for the restoration was also a problem in itself. The project was divided into four phases over a period of six years, which enabled the townhall to more or less function as normal during its restoration. Another reason for the phases was a financial one: funding could now be raised in stages. After 18 months of initial preparation, Van Hoogevest's project was approved by the cultural minister in January 1988. The grant pledged, which at that time was now almost two-and-a-half-million guilders, would be honoured providing the work was started before 1 April 1989. Under pressure from this deadline, Hilversum council then gave the green light in October 1988 for preparing the contracting out of the first phase. It was still unsure if this phase would, in fact, be carried out and even less unsure whether the council would approve the subsequent phases.

Funding and realisation

The decision to start the work was taken during a Hilversum council meeting of 11 January 1989. On this occasion there was a reasonable detailed overview of the four phases with their corresponding budget, which was split into unavoidable and possibly deferrable costs. For the time being only the necessary work would be carried out, put a total estimate of some 27 million guilders. According to the calculations of the ministry responsible for historic buildings conservation, the town hall was eligible for a grant of just over ten-and-a-half-million guilders. The council was expected to foot the rest of the bill and this could be done by spending two million guilders of investment capital annually on the town hall over an eight-year period. The council decided in principle to make the total investment themselves and to put up the money for the first phase. Each subsequent phase would then be put to the council again.

In dealing with the issue, the council was broadly unanimous concerning the inevitability of the operation. Only one council member from the Christian Democrats had suggested selling the town hall and building a less monumental building, but this was never taken really seriously. The councillors were worried, however, about the costs possibly running out of hand or grants for subsequent phases not being forthcoming. For this reason they wanted to take the first step cautiously without taking on any obligations of which the consequences would only be known later. This first modest step clearly set the wheels of train in motion. It would from then on be difficult (or costly) to stop it.

During the first phase the tower, reception hall and east office wing were restored, including the set of bells. A new clock appeared, named after the cultural minister of the day, Elco Brinkman. The council's fears concerning the approving of the second phase were well founded. According to the figures of Historic Buildings Conservation, the state this time should provide funding of just under four million guilders, but this came to nothing more than a vague promise of two million. In order to get out of the impasse, the City manager of Hilversum P.L. Polhuis came up with the idea to sent a traditional marzipan treat in the form of a town hall around the time of the feast of St Nicholas in December 1990 to all MPs along with a letter from the council executive committee. This gesture was a popular one, as a Christian Democrat party motion to allocate the extra two mil-lion pounds proves. It was given overwhelming support. With this final payment, it would to be left at that, despite the fact that there were two more phases lined up. Together with a grant of 600,000 guilders from North Holland county coun-cil things were not too bad and the second phase could begin. This included the restoration of the north wing and the wedding room.

During this period, the council sought advice from Starke Diekstra, a firm of consultants, who thought the restoration programme had been drawn up in a fitting, well-conceived and balanced way and that there was actually no other alternative. In the event that the state would not provide any further funding, Starke Diekstra suggested the possibility of using the money reserved by the council for the restoration for carrying out the third phase as far as was possible. The fourth phase, that is the outbuildings and garden, would then have to be postponed.

The restoration became a real concern when the vital third phase had to be made ready. The council asked Historic Buildings Conservation Department for five million guilders while the two million guilder grant from phase two had not yet been received. This situation made it risky for the council to continue, for without new funding a deficit of millions of guilders loomed. On the other hand, suspending restoration had limited appeal seeing that retaining the building site would cost at least 70,000 guilders a month; money that was being thrown away in fact. Put on the spot, the council executive committee came up with an emergency mea-

Clock in council executive committee room

sure. Phase three was to be namely split into two parts so that the council with a loan of five million guilders for Phase 3A could gain time to organise a lobby for the six-and-a-half million needed for phase 3B. A further benefit to this was that in this phase the two remaining office wings could be vacated and moved to each other, which made temporary accommodation easier. Again the council could do little more than agree to this. Mrs Lamaker-Willemars from the Hilversum 2000 party thought that it should all be far less luxurious and proposed finding extra money through sponsoring. The other councillors were nanimous, however, that there should be no economising on standards and that, in the words of Councillor Kuijper, representing the reformed political association, *sponsoring was all right for a zoo but not for a town hall'*.

While the restoration could continue for the time being, the council made a last-ditch attempt to get more funding. To this end, an appeal was lodged with the Council of State against the decision not to award the requested five million guilders. The council argued that by approving the restoration, the cultural minister had allied himself to the entire project and it was thus unreasonable to opt out half way through. At the end of 1992 everything was finally straightened out. First the new cultural minister Hedy d'Ancona came up with the missing two million guilders for the second phase, then a deal was reached which gave a final grant of four million guilders. Together with the council's investments and by tapping other sources for instance for furniture, fixtures and fittings and relocation, there was suddenly money for the remaining phases and even for several other refurbishments, such as the garden, which had at first been put on ice. Ultimately, due to extra spending and rising prices, the cost of the restoration still came to 32 million guilders.

Technical aspects

Although the town hall was still virtually intact, much new work had to be made. Three quarters of the exterior walls were replaced, 80 per cent of the windows were reproduced, while the upper 14 metres of the tower is a replica. In most instances, such drastic measures were the only way of correcting building defects and doing justice to the architectonic image. The new brickwork has been fired hard, for instance, dilated at regular points and separated from the inner wall by a small cavity. After a long search, a German brick manufacturer was able to make the desired brick. During the first phase of the restoration all the bricks needed for the entire project had already been produced in one firing process in order to prevent colour nuances. The new, polyethylene drainpipes can no longer rust through the walls, while the danger of blockage seems to have been averted by using another type of bituminous roofing material.

The manufacturer of the mouldings from which the steel window frames were constructed was traced to England and was still able to produce the required material. As with the bricks, during the first phase all the window mouldings were bought at once. In order to retain the original detailing the windows still have single glass though certain of the office windows have had secondary glazing added to exclude draughts. Virtually all the technical installations were renewed. Above the ceilings there was space to take, among others, a modern ventilation system and information network. Where installations are visible they have been executed as far as possible in a 'Dudok' style. The requirement of adding fire exits in the corridors was quite a drastic measure, but by making them of glass at least the square can still be experienced. An extra passenger lift was a further addition to the building.

Functional aspects

User friendly is a concept that in Dudok's day did not then have its present significance. In other words there was plenty of scope for creating a recognisable public entrance, a well thought out reception area and new signposting. Around the entrance on *Hoge Naarderweg* a corner of the square was designated as a reception area with a reception desk. The marble revolving door was abandoned for a Dudok-type swinging door. Elsewhere in the building this type of revolving door was preserved. The new reception area was designed in keeping with the rest of the building and has, among others, built-in cupboards. The desk stands on a black plinth and has a cherry wood work surface. New Dudok style reception desks were placed in the Civic Affairs department. During restoration the design for this department had to be modified due to new guidelines for safeguarding the issuing of passports. As far as this department was concerned, the overall increase in town hall personnel could be solved by incorporating the cellar. This created a sequence of nine new windows at ground level along the open courtyard. Not all the building had originally been above a cellar. Van Hoogevest proposed digging out the rest and thereby gaining 200 square metres for technical spaces and archives, exhibition space or even a Dudok museum. During the critical period of trying to balance the finances for the third phase, this extension was scrapped from the programme but the council rescinded this cutback. For 160.000 guilders the space was too good an opportunity to lose.

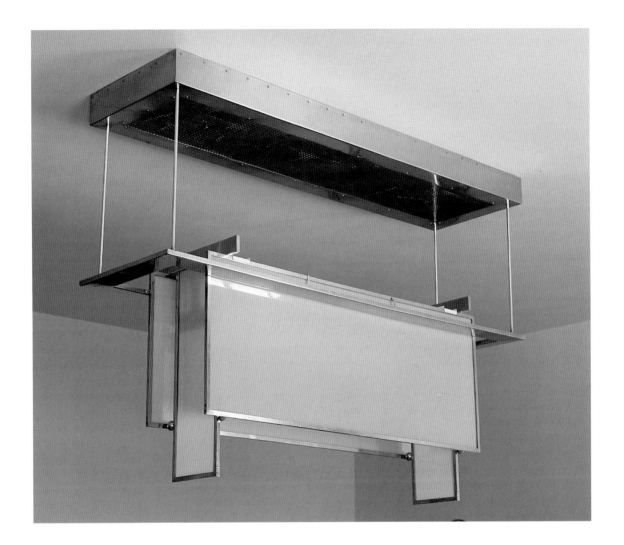

Lamp in the council executive committee room

[46]   *Dudok's office*
        Council executive committee room

Colour and interior

A surprising aspect of the restoration was the use of colour. Due to there being no colour photographs of the building shortly after it was built, Dudok's palette had to be established from traces of paint. The discovery of ochre paint on the steel windows created a stir as everyone assumed they had always been white. There was also more evidence that yellow had been used originally. In the extension there were still a few yellow-painted steel doors which had probably been overlooked during re-painting. Other evidence was an elevation on a scale of 1:20 in which the window frames are clearly identified in yellow and the windowsills in white. Yellow was once more reinstated during the restoration, also for the interior where an examination for paint traces revealed that several shades of yellow were used for its walls. Behind the panelling applied later in the main hall the yellow paint was still visible. Precisely the same shade was behind the plaque of Queen Wilhelmina. The original colours were scanned and mixed again.

Colour was also a cause for concern regarding the restoration and reconstruction of the soft furnishings and furniture. As far as possible an attempt was made to find hard evidence of the original, for instance, by searching for old material remnants. Certain new spaces such as the garden room were designed in the style of the rest of the building. The mayoral chamber was reconstructed down to the last detail. In the council chamber a new table was made for the members which was both broader and longer to provide space for all the paperwork and for the increased number of councillors nowadays. The old one was put to use elsewhere in the building. The offices were furnished according to modern standards, including the proper illumination of workspaces (ARBO regulations). Modern security devices against fire, burglary and hold-ups were also installed. Even up-to-the-minute gadgetry was used outside the building, such as underfloor heating for the exterior steps to prevent slipping in cold weather, while there is a computer-assisted sprinkling system in the garden enabling it to operate automatically.

A remarkable project?

The town hall's restoration was undoubtedly a success. From a technical and art historical viewpoint there was widespread agreement among the specialists. There was no budget overspending and failures were kept to a minimum. For instance it was impossible to remove brown teak oil stains from the marble despite the assistance of Italian specialists. A second minus point was that no original electricity switches could be found that confirmed to present-day safety standards. Thus the town hall now has few 'Dudok' switches. Yet for such a complex and all-embracing project, the teak oil and the switches, no matter how important they may seem, are obviously negligible details.

Surprises and 'finds' which can be spectacular with some restoration or building work (for instance the Heren van Amstel castle in Amsterdam) were limited to the town hall cellar and attic. When digging out the cellar the foundations of *Witten Hull* villa were discovered. This can now partly be seen. In the attic, bombs, grenades and German signposts were unearthed, a reminder of the time when the town hall was the military head quarters of the occupying power.